Dr. Seuss Workbook
KINDERGARTEN

Contents

READING

EXPLORE YOUR WORLD!

Throughout this book, you'll find activity pages that encourage kids to learn and explore everywhere. These pages don't follow the specific learning goals of the lessons. They are meant to expand learning beyond the book, sending kids searching, counting, and crafting all around the house—and even outside!

MATH

FEELINGS

SCIENCE

Dear Parents,

There's a world of learning inside the pages of this workbook, and your child will get the most out of it with your support. Here are some tips:

- Encourage your child. Positivity is important, especially when your child finds a task frustrating or difficult!

- Make sure your child has a quiet, comfortable place to work.

- Read the activity directions with your child.

- Give your child a variety of colored pencils and markers to write down the answers and draw pictures.

- Check your child's answers and gently guide your child to the correct response if it wasn't his or her first choice.

- Spend extra time with your child on the areas that he or she finds difficult.

- Pull out your child's best work and display the pages around your home.

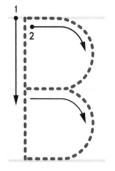

This book uses a system of dots and arrows for children to follow for letter tracing activities.

Each black dot (•) indicates the beginning of a new line, where the pen should leave the page to make a separate stroke. The arrows (→) show the direction of pen movement. Strokes without numbers indicate a continuation and change of direction.

READING →

The more that you READ, the more things you'll KNOW. The more that you LEARN, the more places you'll GO.

Collect your stickers at the end of each lesson.

The Letters A–J

Do you want to read?

You're on your way!

Just color the letters from A a to J j.

A a

B b

C c

D d

Ee

Ff

Gg

Hh

Ii

Jj

7

The Letter A

Trace, then write uppercase A.

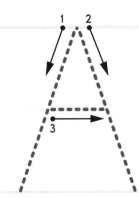

Trace, then write lowercase a.

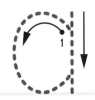

Circle the thing that starts with the letter A.

The Letter B

Trace, then write uppercase **B**.

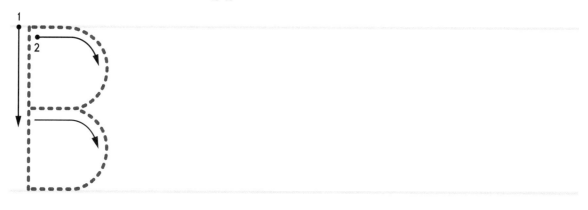

Trace, then write lowercase **b**.

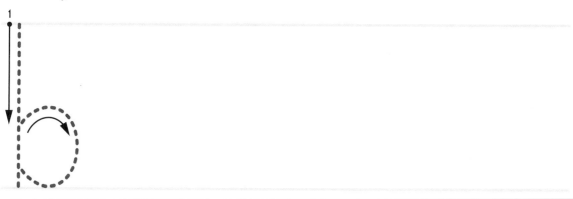

Color the things that start with the letter **B**.

The Letter C

Trace, then write uppercase C.

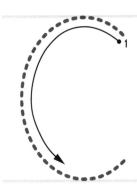

Trace, then write lowercase c.

Circle the things that start with the letter C.

Cc

The Letter D

Trace, then write uppercase D.

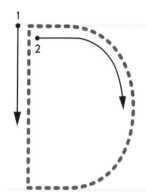

Trace, then write lowercase d.

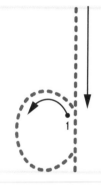

D

Draw a path from the letter **D** to the thing that starts with **D**.

The Letter E

Trace, then write uppercase **E**.

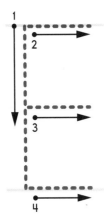

Trace, then write lowercase **e**.

Circle the thing that starts with the letter **E**.

The Letter F

Trace, then write uppercase **F**.

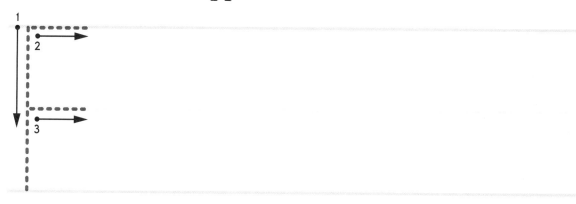

Trace, then write lowercase **f**.

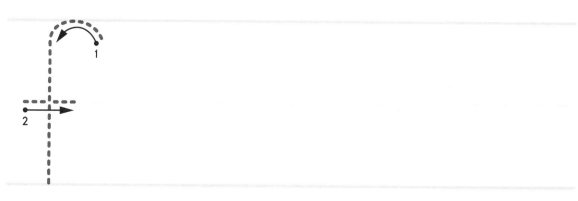

Color the thing that starts with the letter **F**.

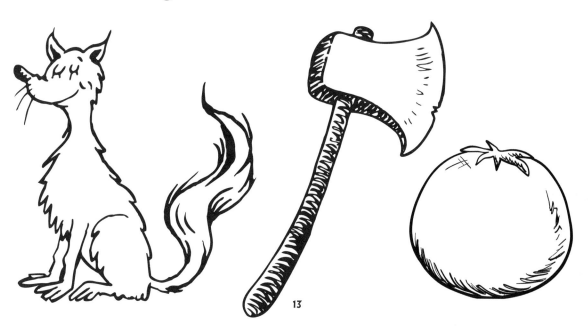

13

The Letter G

Trace, then write uppercase **G**.

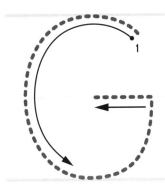

Trace, then write lowercase **g**.

Circle the things that start with the letter **G**.

Gg

The Letter H

Trace, then write uppercase H.

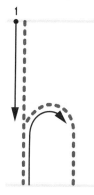

Trace, then write lowercase h.

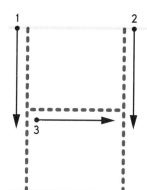

Draw a path from the letter H to the thing that starts with the letter H.

The Letter I

Trace, then write uppercase I.

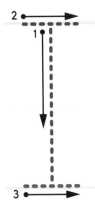

Trace, then write lowercase i.

Circle the thing that starts with the letter I.

The Letter J

Trace, then write uppercase J.

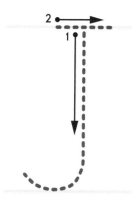

Trace, then write lowercase j.

Color the thing that starts with the letter J.

The Letters A–J

Letter Hunt

If you look close enough, there are letters all around you. Point to a letter C hidden in the picture. What other letters can you find? Circle them.

Now go on a letter hunt around the house or outside with a friend or family member. How many hidden letters can you find?

The Letters K–T

Here are ten more letters.
We'll start with the letter K.

Name each one, and then
make the sounds they say!

Draw a line from each
uppercase letter to its
lowercase partner.

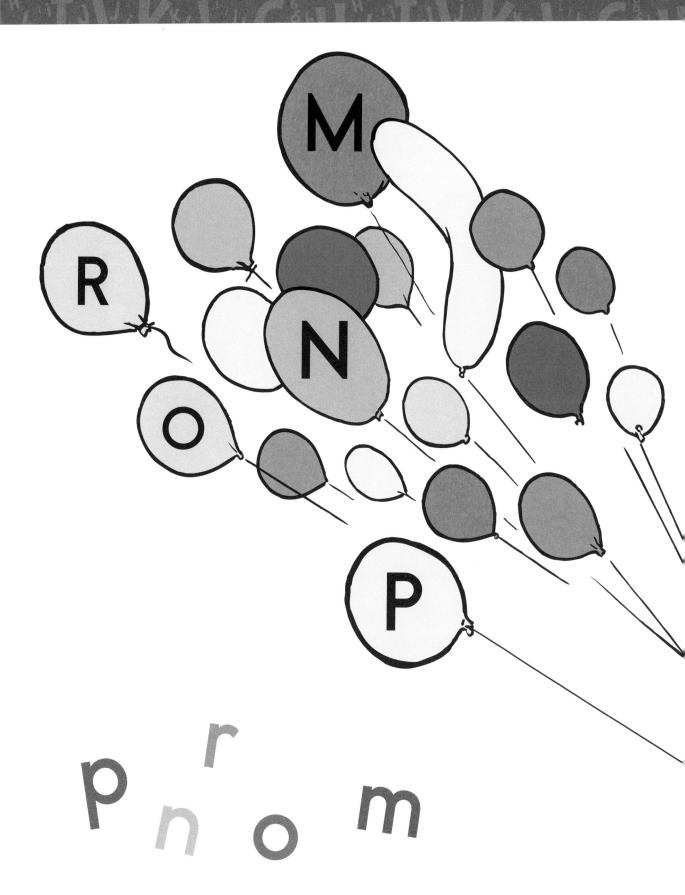

The Letter K

Trace, then write uppercase K.

Trace, then write lowercase k.

K

Draw a path from the letter K to the thing that starts with the letter K.

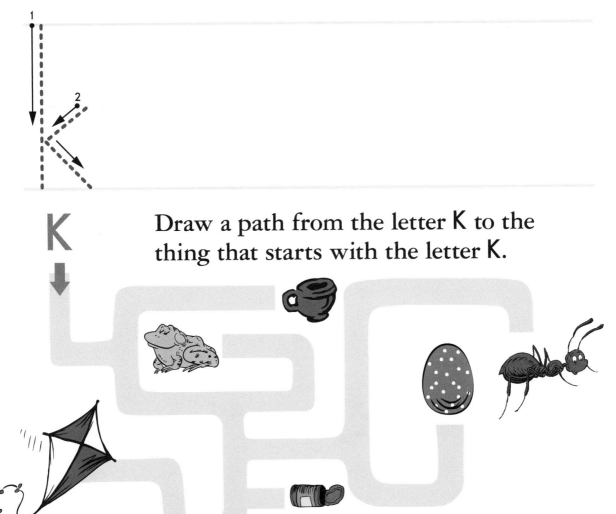

The Letter L

Trace, then write uppercase L.

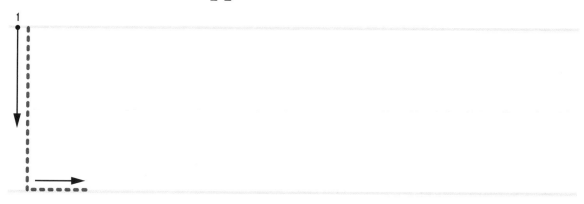

Trace, then write lowercase l.

Circle the things that start with the letter L.

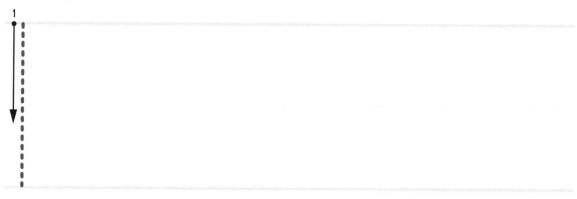

The Letter M

Trace, then write uppercase M.

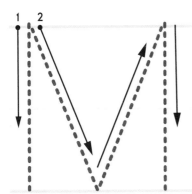

Trace, then write lowercase m.

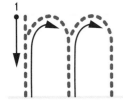

Circle the thing that starts with the letter M.

The Letter N

Trace, then write uppercase N.

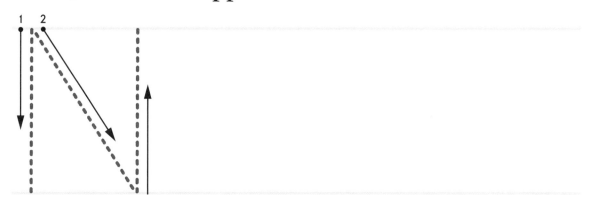

Trace, then write lowercase n.

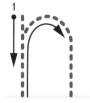

Color the things that start with the letter N.

The Letter O

Trace, then write uppercase O.

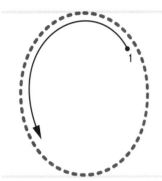

Trace, then write lowercase o.

Circle the things that start with the letter O.

The Letter P

Trace, then write uppercase **P**.

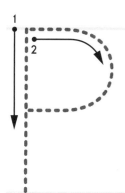

Trace, then write lowercase **p**.

P

Draw a path from the letter **P** to the thing that starts with the letter **P**.

The Letter Q

Trace, then write uppercase **Q**.

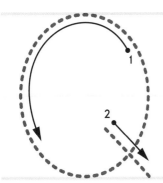

Trace, then write lowercase **q**.

Color the thing that starts with the letter **Q**.

The Letter R

Trace, then write uppercase R.

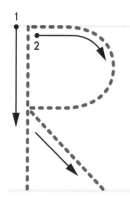

Trace, then write lowercase r.

Circle the thing that starts with the letter R.

The Letter S

Trace, then write uppercase **S**.

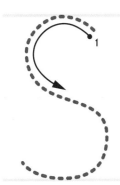

Trace, then write lowercase **s**.

Circle the things that start with the letter S.

The Letter T

Trace, then write uppercase T.

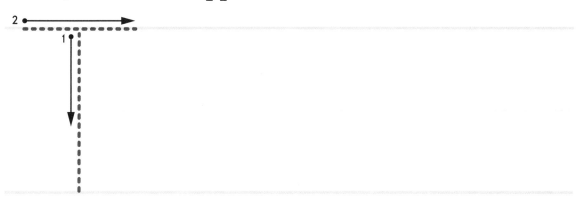

Trace, then write lowercase t.

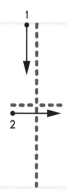

Draw a path from the letter T to the thing that starts with the letter T.

The Letters K-T

The Letters U-Z

You're almost at the end, let's see.
The end of the alphabet is from **U** to **Z**.

Trace a path that goes from
U to **V**, to **W**, **X**, **Y**, and **Z**.

Write the letters below in the correct order
in which they appear in the alphabet.

Z U Y X V W

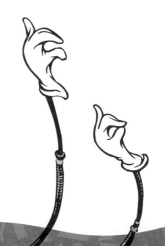

The Letter U

Trace, then write uppercase U.

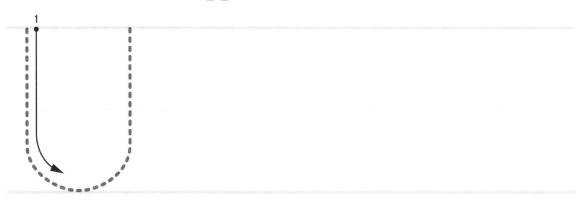

Trace, then write lowercase u.

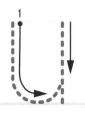

Circle the thing that starts with the letter U.

The Letter V

Trace, then write uppercase V.

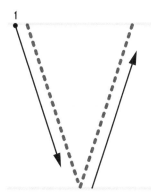

Trace, then write lowercase v.

Color the thing that starts with the letter V.

The Letter W

Trace, then write uppercase **W**.

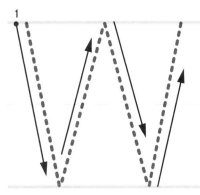

Trace, then write lowercase **w**.

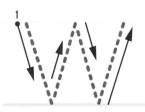

Circle the things that start with the letter **W**.

The Letter X

Trace, then write uppercase **X**.

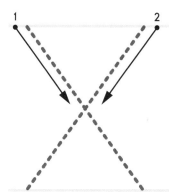

Trace, then write lowercase **x**.

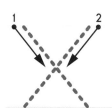

X

Draw a path from the letter **X** to the thing that starts with the letter **X**.

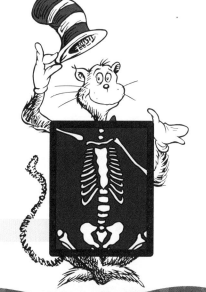

The Letter Y

Trace, then write uppercase Y.

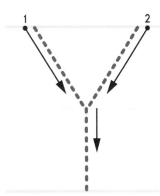

Trace, then write lowercase y.

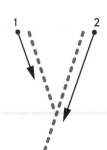

Color the thing that starts with the letter Y.

The Letter Z

Trace, then write uppercase **Z**.

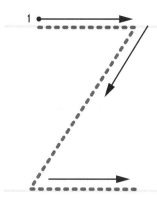

Trace, then write lowercase **z**.

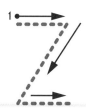

Circle the thing that starts with the letter **Z**.

The Letters U–Z

Words with Short Vowels

There are five special letters:
A, E, I, O, and U.

We call them vowels.
Do you know what they can do?

They can make more than
one sound—listen to
pup, **pot**, and **pen**.

We'll learn short vowel
sounds now. And later,
we'll meet vowels again.

Trace, then write the letters **a**, **e**, **i**, **o**, and **u**.

Color all the balloons with vowels.

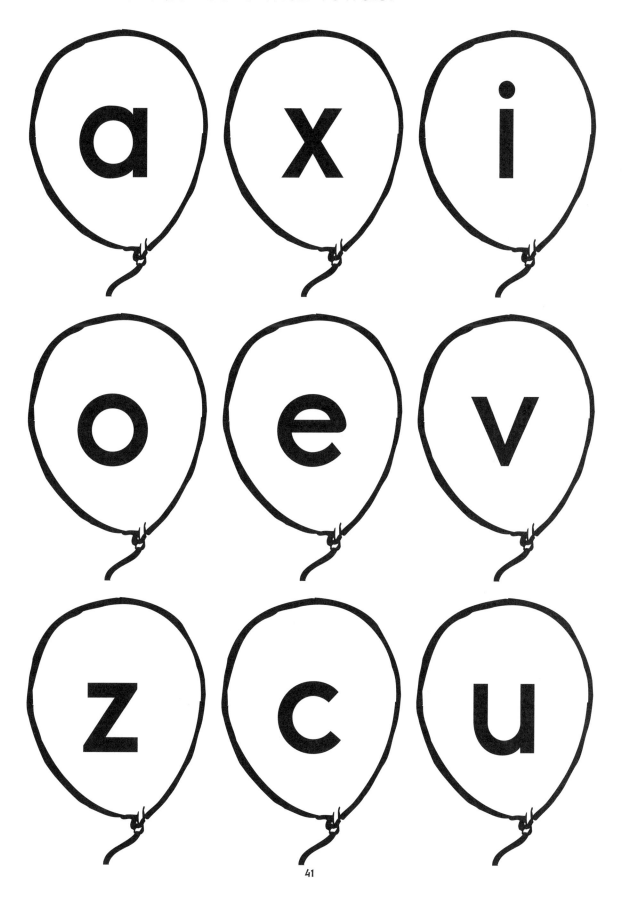

Words with a Short A

The word **map** has the short **a** sound in the middle.

Write the letter **a** to finish each word, then say the word aloud.

What sound does the letter **a** make?

s___t

p___n

b___t

___xe

Color four things that have a short **a** sound.

Words with a Short E

The word **bed** has the short **e** sound in the middle.

Write the letter **e** to finish each word, then say the word aloud.

What sound does the letter **e** make?

r____d

v____t

g____m

Circle three things that have a short **e** sound.

Words with a Short I

The word **pig** has the short i sound in the middle.

Write the letter i to finish each word, then say the word aloud.

What sound does the letter i make?

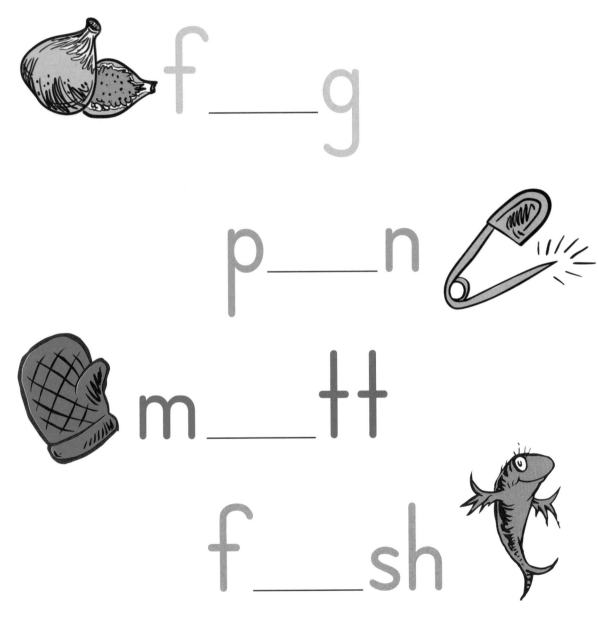

f___g

p___n

m___tt

f___sh

Draw paths to the words with a short i sound.

sit

pig

fin

pen

dig

hat

Words with a Short o

The word **mom** has the short **o** sound in the middle.

Write the letter **o** to finish each word, then say the word aloud.

What sound does the letter **o** make?

d____g

cl____ck

h____lly

h____p

Circle the word for each thing with a short **o** sound.

tag

top

tin

box

bit

bot

fix

fox

for

pam

pat

pot

Words with a Short U

The word **bug** has the short **u** sound in the middle.

Write the letter **u** to finish each word, then say the word aloud.

What sound does the letter **u** make?

tr____ck

p____p

b____g

Color three things that have a short u sound.

More Short Vowels

Look at each thing. Write the missing vowel in each word.

f___n

 b___d

p___g

f___x

c___p

Circle the word for each thing.

pan

pop

net

not

mitt

mop

sun

sap

Words with Short Vowels

The Other Sounds of Letters

Other letters are special, like **Y**, **C**, and **G**. They make more than one sound—do you know what they might be?

C can make a soft sound like **S**.
G can make a soft sound like **J**.
Y can make a vowel sound like **E** and **I**.

C → S
G → J
Y → E/I

Look at each thing and say its name.

Color the thing with a soft c sound blue. Color the thing with a soft g sound green. Color the thing where y sounds like a vowel red.

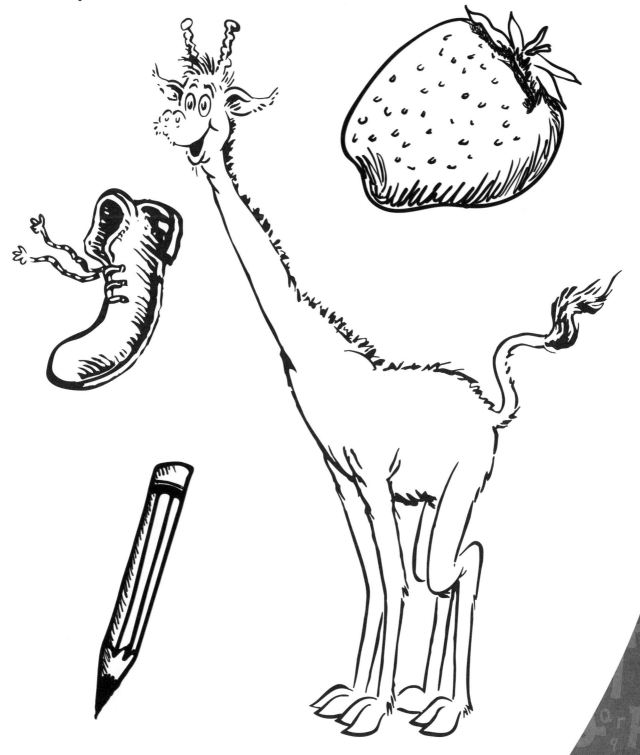

Words with a Soft c

The letter **c** can make a hard sound, as in **cat**.

The letter **c** can make a soft sound, as in **cereal**.

cat

cereal

Look at each thing and say its name.

If the word starts with a hard c sound, circle the letter k. If the word starts with a soft c sound, circle the letter s.

celery

k   s

cake

k   s

coins

k   s

corn

k   s

Words with a Soft G

The letter **g** can make a hard sound, as in **goat**.

The letter **g** can make a soft sound, as in **gem**.

goat

gem

Look at each thing and say its name.

Circle the things that start with a soft **g** sound.

Words with Y as a Vowel

The letter y can make a long **e** sound, as in **baby**.

The letter y can make a long i sound, as in **fly**.

baby

fly

Look at each thing and say its name.

If the word ends with an **e** sound, circle the letter **e**.

If the word ends with an i sound, circle the letter i.

butterfly

e   i

bunny

e   i

strawberry

e   i

cry

e   i

The Other Sounds of Letters

61

BOOM

Bim, Bam, Boom!

Can you write the sounds of these noisy pigs? There's a bang and a boom! Write three more sounds they are making.

Now find your own sound makers. Use a pot, a pan, some sticks, and more. How many different sounds can you invent? Write their sounds down, too.

Long Vowels

Remember those letters, A, E, and I? They have more sounds to show you, so give them a try.

Say each word, then write a lowercase **e** at the end.

can_____

cap_____

star_____

kit___

pan___

pin___

Sam___

tap___

Now say each new word.
How did the vowel sound change?

A as in "Cake"

Do you hear the **a** in **lake** and **tape**?

Color each thing that uses a long **a** sound.

Unscramble the letters and write the word that matches the thing. Use the word box to help you.

a e k r

e v s a

k c a e

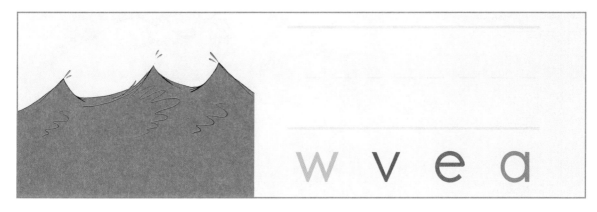

w v e a

AI and AY

The letter **a** partners with other letters to make a long **a** sound.

The letters **ai** make the long **a** sound in **train**.

The letters **ay** make the long **a** sound in **hay**.

train

hay

Write **ai** or **ay** to finish each word.

n___l

p___nt

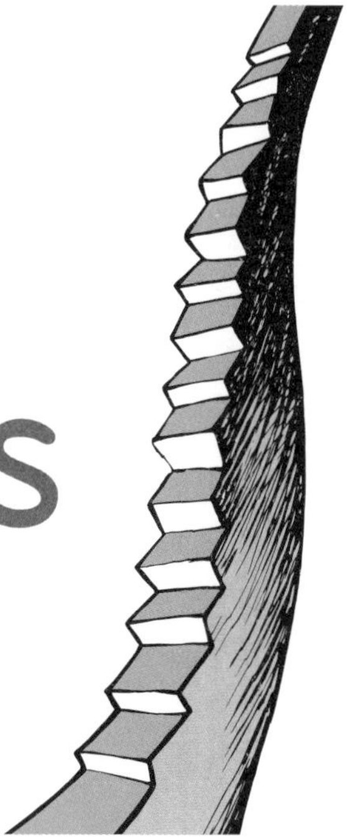

st___rs

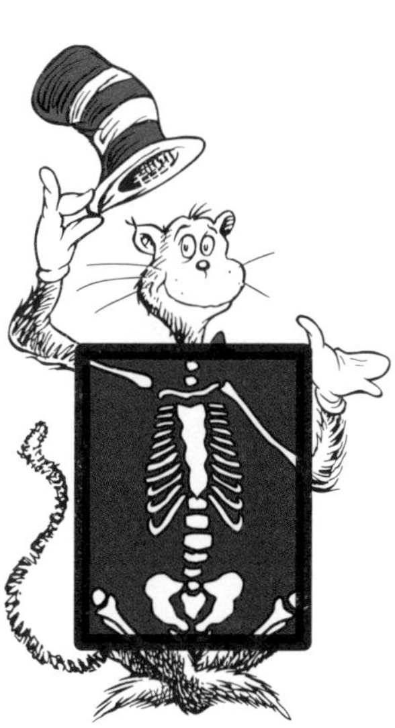

X-r___

EA, EE, and EY

The letter **e** partners with other letters to make a long **e** sound.

The letters **ea** make the long **e** sound in **bean**.

The letters **ee** make the long **e** sound in **tree**.

The letters **ey** make the long **e** sound in **key**.

bean

tree

key

Color each thing that has a long **e** sound.

I as in "Kite"

Hi! Can you hear the long i sound in **bike** and **fire**?

Color each thing that makes the long i sound.

Look at each word. You can make new words by changing the first letter. Write a new word on each line.

hide

r_____

t_____

s_____

w_____

dine

f_____

v_____

l_____

m_____

dime

l_____

ch_____

t_____

sl_____

bike

h_____

l_____

p_____

sp_____

IE and IGH

The letter i partners with other letters to make a long i sound.

The letters **ie** make the long i sound in **pie**.

The letters **igh** make the long i sound in **light**.

pie

light

Write **ie** or **igh** to finish each word.

t_____

kn_____t

h_____

Long Vowels

More Long Vowels

Don't forget those two vowels named O and U.

They also have long sounds, so you know what to do!

Shout their sounds aloud, even if you're alone.

They're in the words **bone**, **cube**, and **phone**!

Color all the things that make either the long **o** sound or the long **u** sound.

O as in "Bone"

Oh, do you hear the long **o** sound in **hope** and **rose**?

Color each thing that makes the long **o** sound.

Unscramble the letters and write
the word that matches the thing.
Use the word box to help you.

e o s r

b e n o

t n e o

m o e h

OA and OW

The letter **o** partners with other letters to make a long **o** sound.

The letters **oa** make the long **o** sound in **soap**.

The letters **ow** make the long **o** sound in **row**.

soap

row

Color each thing that has a long o sound.

U as in "Tube"

Can you hear the long u in **mule** and **tube**?

Color each thing that makes the long u sound.

cube

t_____

tune

J_____

mule

r_____

cute

fl_____

Look at the word in each box. On the line below, use the given first letter to create a word that rhymes.

Now make up a song using the rhymes.

UE and UI

The letter **u** partners with other letters to make a long **u** sound.

The letters **ue** make the long **u** sound in **blue**.

The letters **ui** make the long **u** sound in **suit**.

blue

suit

Write **ue** or **ui** to finish each word.

fr_____t

gl_____

j_____ce

More Long Vowels

EXPLORE **YOUR** WORLD!

Hop! Skip! Jump!

How many rocks long is the path? Write the measurement here: _____ rocks.

Use your body to measure things. How many hands long is your bed? How many footsteps long is your room? If someone else in your family measures the same thing the same way, is the measurement the same or different? Why?

Letters Work Together

Some letters pair up to make sounds that are new. Like **GR**, and **BR**, and **CL**, too!

Draw a circle around the first two letters of each word. Say the sound they make.

grapes

clock

brick

truck

Each of these words starts with a letter pair.
Say each word aloud using a different voice for each one.

block

snake

flip

stop

plus

brow

slip

crab

clock

brick

trip

smog

drip

frog

Words with BL, CL, and FL

Circle the letter pair that starts each word.

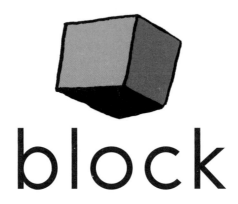

block

clown

flower

Draw a line from each word to the thing it matches.

black

blanket

cloud

flag

clock

Words with PL and SL

Circle the letter pair that starts each word.

plant

sled

slug

Circle the word that matches each thing.

pull

plum

slug

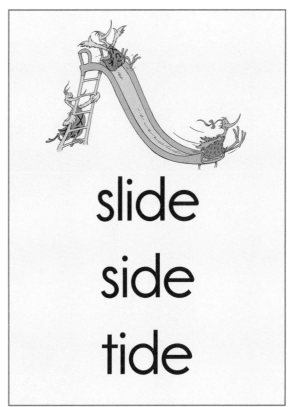

slide

side

tide

slipper

flipper

dipper

rake

plan

play

Words with BR, CR, and DR

Circle the letter pair that starts each word.

bread

crab

dress

Write the letters **br**, **cr**, or **dr** to start each word.

broom

crown

drum

Words with FR, GR, and TR

Circle the letter pair that starts each word.

frog

grass

tree

Draw a line from each word to the thing it matches.

frown

train

grapes

truck

green

fruit

Words with SM, SN, and SP

Circle the letter pair that starts each word.

smile

snail

spider

Circle the word that matches each thing.

stoke

smoke

snake

moon

snow

spoon

spree

snake

breeze

win

spine

spin

Words with ST and STR

Circle the letter pairs that start each word.

star

stop

strawberry

Write the letters **st** or **str** to start each word.

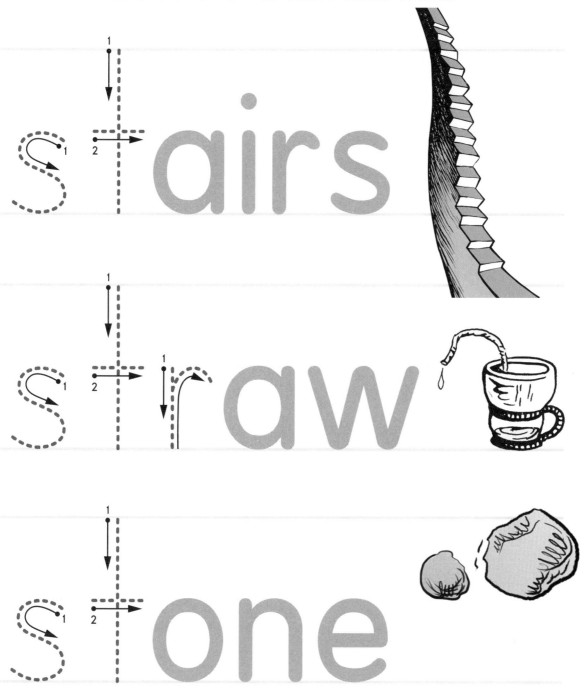

stairs

straw

stone

Letters Work Together

101

sh wh ph
th ch

More Letters Together

With a P and an H, you can make
the word **phone**. And it starts with
a sound that they don't make alone.

Draw a circle around the first two letters
of each word. Say the sound they make.

chair

phone

shoe

thin

whale

Read each word, then say the single sound the first two letters make.

cheese

photo

ship

thorn

wheat

shirt

chair

phone

shower

whale

sheep

thumb

thin

chalk

shoe

three

queen

103

Words with CH

Say the sound the letters
ch make together.

chick

chase

couch

104

Color the things that begin with a **ch** sound.

Words with SH

Say the sound the letters sh make together.

shower

shovel

shoe

106

Circle the word that matches each thing.

sheep

sleep

seal

ship

sip

flip

capes

apes

shapes

spark

shark

mark

Words with TH

Say the sound the letters th make together.

Earth

father

bath

Write the letters **th** to complete each word.

thumb

mother

teeth

Words with PH and WH

Say the sound the letters **ph** make together.

photo

elephant

phone

Say the sound the letters **wh** make together.

wheel

whisker

whisk

Words with QU

Say the sound the letters
qu make together.

queen

quiet

quack

Circle the word that matches each thing.

quilt

silt

guilt

cart

quick

quiet

tail

pail

quill

quarter

brother

marker

More Letters Together

Beautiful Dreamer

This dreamer is traveling to a new world in his sleep. Where is he going? Who will he meet? Write a sentence to tell about his dream.

Keep a piece of paper and a pencil or crayon next to your bed. The next time you wake up and remember your dream, draw a picture and write words to record it.

Sight Words

you he I

her me us

Some letters form words you can sound out just right.

But some, you must memorize—learn them by sight.

Read the words and memorize what they look like. Then write a sentence using at least two of them.

I   they

you	me
he	him
she	her
it	us
we	them

Pronouns: I, You, He, She, It, We, They

I like tweetle beetles.
You like tweetle beetles.
He likes tweetle beetles.
She likes tweetle beetles.
It likes tweetle beetles.
We like tweetle beetles.
They like tweetle beetles.

Pick a pronoun, a verb, and an noun from each column to make a sentence.

I	push(es)	bugs
You	hold(s)	pigs

He	paint(s)	fleas
She	wash(es)	dogs
It	drive(s)	ducks
We	ride(s)	pans
They	like(s)	bikes

Pronouns: Me, You, Him, Her, It, Us, Them

Tweetle beetles fight **me**.
Tweetle beetles fight **you**.
Tweetle beetles fight **him**.
Tweetle beetles fight **her**.
Tweetle beetles fight **it**.
Tweetle beetles fight **us**.
Tweetle beetles fight **them**.

Circle the pronoun that correctly finishes each sentence.

A noodle-eating poodle meets (I   we   us).

Pop hops on (he   it   she).

Sally and (I her us)
don't like bugs.

Can (you him us)
blow a bubble?

Did (them we us)
run out of ink?

them

Verbs: Am, Is, Are, Do, Does, Have, Has

Verbs are action words.

am
is
are
do
does
have
has

Pick a pronoun, a verb, and an word from each column to make a sentence.

I	am	tall
You	are	small
He	is	happy

She	does	silly
It	do	clocks
We	has	dishes
They	have	work

Sight Words

Certificate of Achievement

★

is presented to

NAME

for becoming a

Remarkable Reader!

MATH

Some have TWO feet, and some have FOUR. Some have SIX feet, and some have MORE.

Collect your stickers at the end of each lesson.

Numbers 1–10

Thing 1 loves **1**,
Thing 2 loves **2**—
counting is so fun to do!
1, 2, 3, right up to **10**—
10, 9, 8, and down again.
Once you practice
counting all the time,
you can count right up
to Thing 99!

Write the number that comes before or after.

1 2 ____

____ 7 ____ 9

4 _____ 6

2 3 _____

_____ 9 10

4 5 _____

6 _____ 8

_____ 3 4

Numbers 1 and 2

Trace, then write the number 1.

Trace, then write the word **one**.

Circle **one** fox.

Trace, then write the number **2**.

Trace, then write the word **two**.

Draw a box around **two** bears.

Numbers 3 and 4

Trace, then write the number **3**.

Trace, then write the word **three**.

Color **three** fish red.

Trace, then write the number 4.

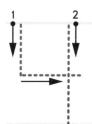

Trace, then write the word **four**.

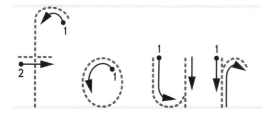

Color **four** fish blue.

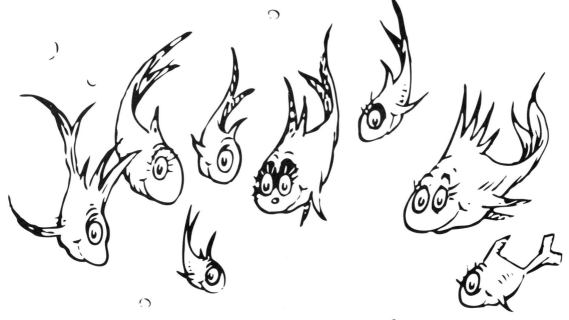

Numbers 5 and 6

Trace, then write the number **5**.

Trace, then write the word **five**.

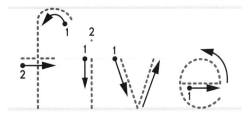

Draw a line from each group of **five** items to the number **5**.

5

132

Trace, then write the number **6**.

Trace, then write the word **six**.

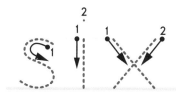

Circle the groups that have **six** items.

Numbers 7 and 8

Trace, then write the number 7.

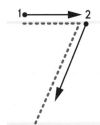

Trace, then write the word **seven**.

Circle **seven** pups.

Trace, then write the number **8**.

Trace, then write the word **eight**.

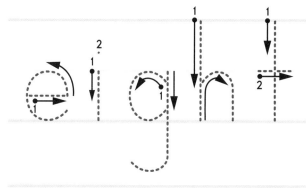

Draw a box around **eight** stars.

Numbers 9 and 10

Trace, then write the number **9**.

Trace, then write the word **nine**.

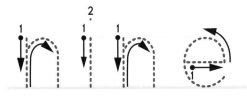

Color **nine** owls orange.

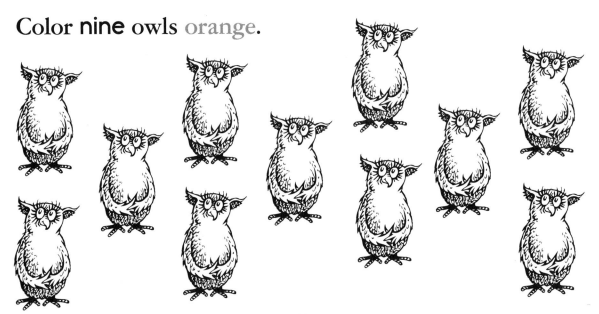

Trace, then write the number **10**.

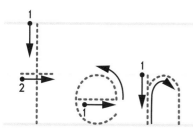

Trace, then write the word **ten**.

Color **ten** balls red.

Numbers 1–10

YOU DID IT!

Count On It!

Two feet, four feet, so many feet to count!
Draw a triangle around someone with two feet.
Draw a square around someone with four feet.
Draw a circle around someone with six feet.

Now let's find other things that come in groups!

In your kitchen, can you find things that come in fours or sixes? Explore other places in your house. Try to find things that come in twos, fives, or tens.

Numbers 11-20

11 12 13 14 15 16 17 18 19 20

Don't stop counting now—
there's much more to go!
The more numbers you count,
the more numbers you'll know!

Write the number that comes before or after.

11 _____ 13

_____ 16 17

18   19   _____

14   15   _____

17   _____   19

12   _____   14

_____   12   13

_____   15   16

Numbers 11 and 12

Trace, then write the number 11.

Trace, then write the word **eleven**.

Draw a line from each group of **eleven** items to the number 11.

Trace, then write the number **12**.

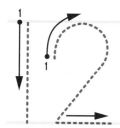

Trace, then write the word **twelve**.

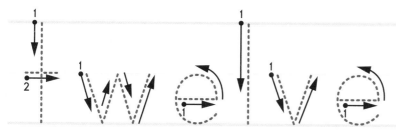

Circle the groups that have **12** items.

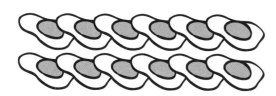

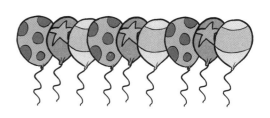

Numbers 13 and 14

Trace, then write the number 13.

Trace, then write the word **thirteen**.

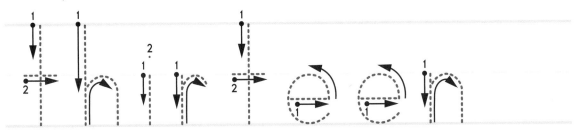

Circle **13** flowers.

Trace, then write the number 14.

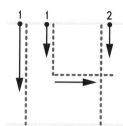

Trace, then write the word **fourteen**.

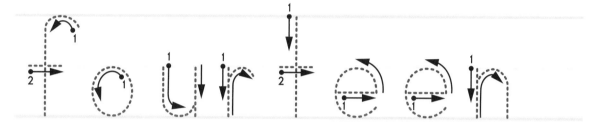

Draw a square around 14 strawberries.

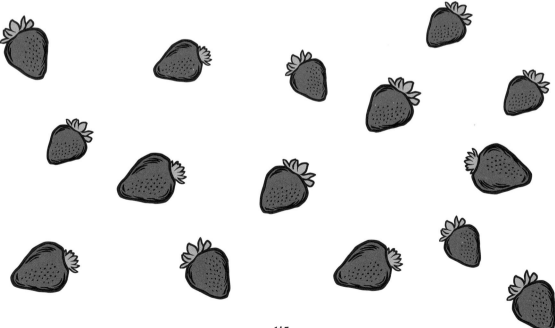

Numbers 15 and 16

Trace, then write the number **15**.

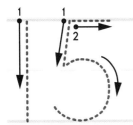

Trace, then write the word **fifteen**.

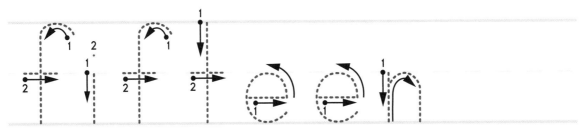

Color 15 balloons orange.

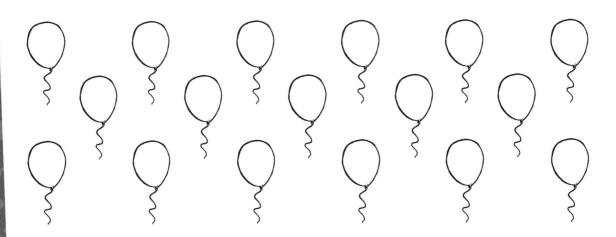

Trace, then write the number **16**.

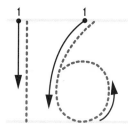

Trace, then write the word **sixteen**.

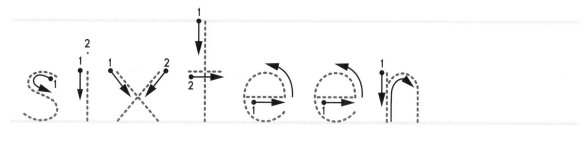

Color **16** beans green.

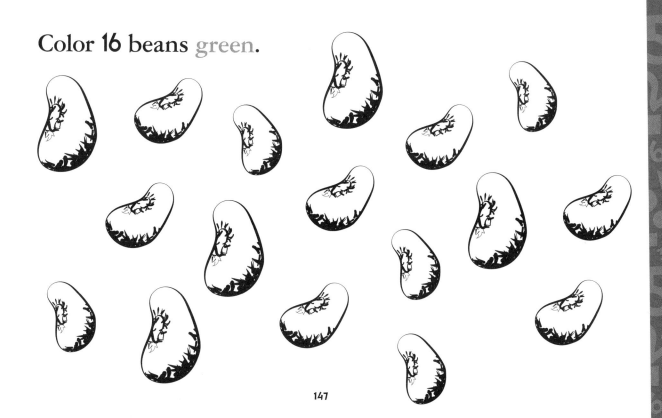

Numbers 17 and 18

Trace, then write the number 17.

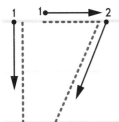

Trace, then write the word **seventeen**.

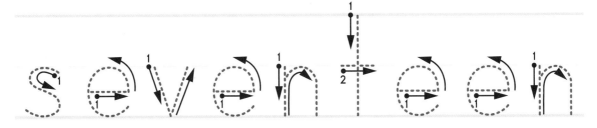

Draw a line from each group of **seventeen** items to the number 17.

17

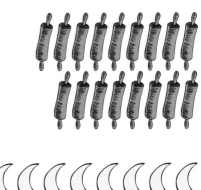

Trace, then write the number **18**.

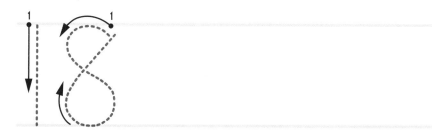

Trace, then write the word **eighteen**.

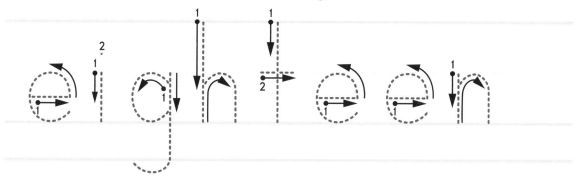

Circle the groups that have **18** items.

Numbers 19 and 20

Trace, then write the number 19.

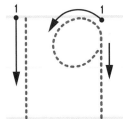

Trace, then write the word **nineteen**.

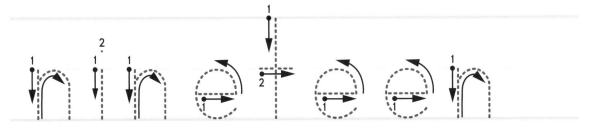

Circle **19** bees.

Trace, then write the number **20**.

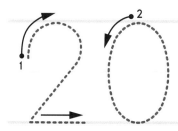

Trace, then write the word **twenty**.

Draw a box around **20** bananas.

Numbers 11–20

YOU DID IT!

Addition

Thing 1 and Thing 2 always love to add—counting makes them gladder than glad. They count those in the first group—they're having a ball! Then they count the next group to find how many in all.

Add the numbers for each group of balls.
Draw how many in all, then write the number.

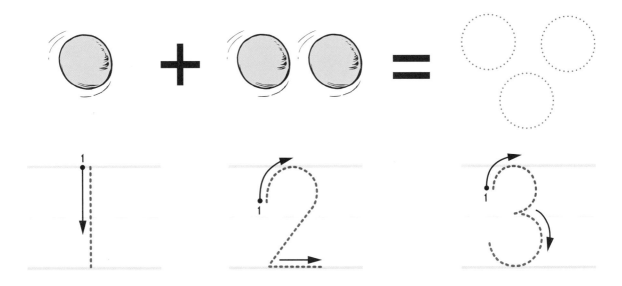

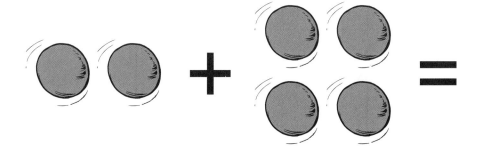

153

How Many in All? (1–5)

Count the items in each group and write the numbers.
Then add them together.

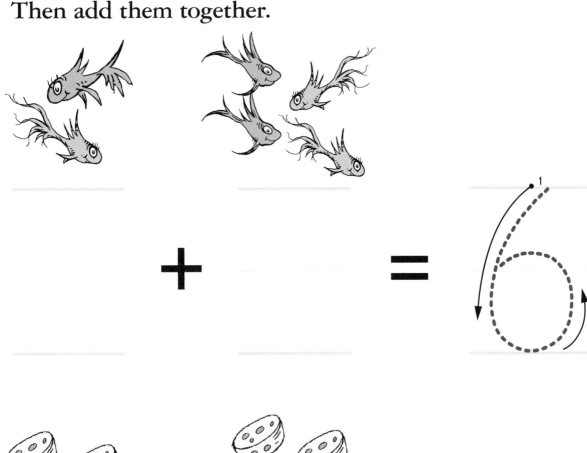

$+$ $=$ 6

$+$ $=$

Add the items, then write the total under each line.

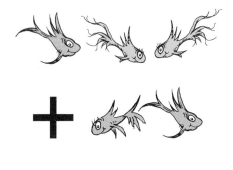 

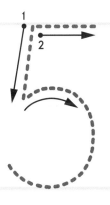

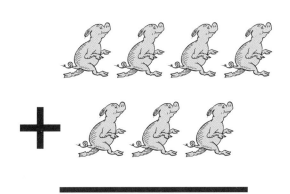 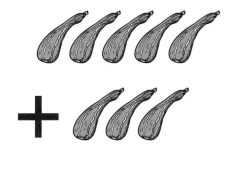

How Many in All? (6-10)

Count the items in each group and write the numbers.
Then add them together.

+   **=**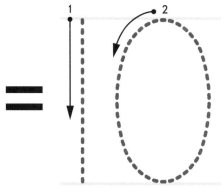

 +   **=**

Add the items, then write the total under each line.

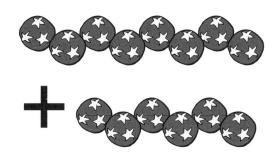

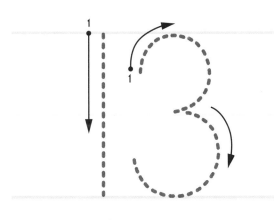

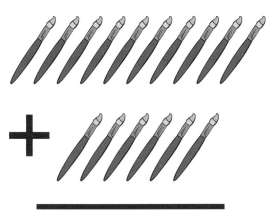

Write the Sums

Add the two numbers together. Then color the picture using the colors that are assigned to each answer.

$$1 + 3 = \underline{}$$

orange

$$3 + 2 = \underline{}$$

red

$$2 + 4 = \underline{}$$

yellow

$$4 + 3 = \underline{}$$

green

$$5 + 3 = \underline{}$$

blue

TICK

TOCK

 **Addition**

Subtraction

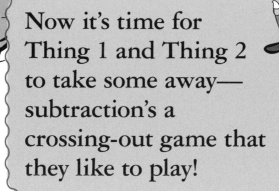

Now it's time for Thing 1 and Thing 2 to take some away— subtraction's a crossing-out game that they like to play!

Count how many items are in each group, then count how many Thing 1 and Thing 2 crossed out. How many items are left?

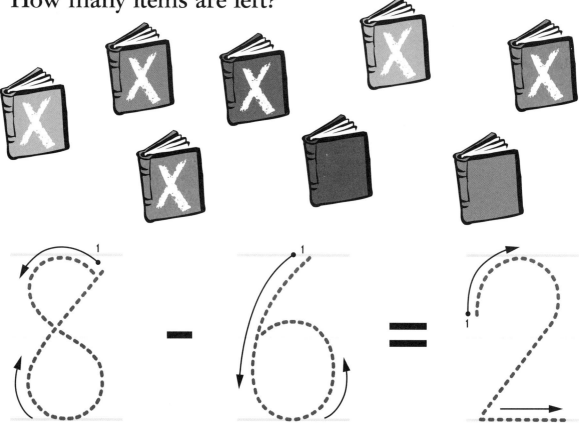

You Did It! Stickers

Place your stickers at the end of each lesson and on your certificates.

READING

MATH

FEELINGS

SCIENCE

—   =

—   =

How Many Are Left? (1–5)

Cross out, then subtract. Write the number of items that are left.

Put an X on **2** hams.

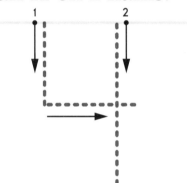

Put an X on **3** balls.

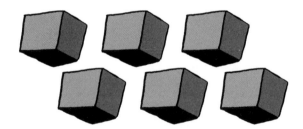

Put an X on **4** cubes.

Put an X on **1** bow.

Subtract the items, then write how many are left under each line.

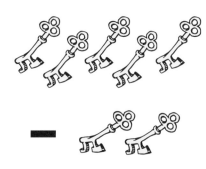

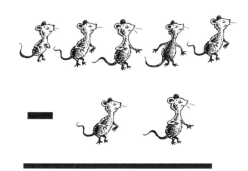

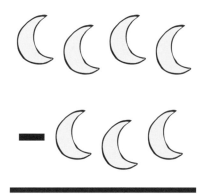

How Many Are Left? (6–10)

Cross out, then subtract. Write the number of items that are left.

Put an X on **3** tomatoes.

Put an X on **2** buckets.

Put an X on **4** light bulbs.

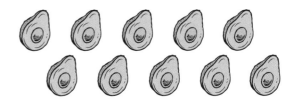

Put an X on **1** avocado.

Subtract the items, then write how many are left under each line.

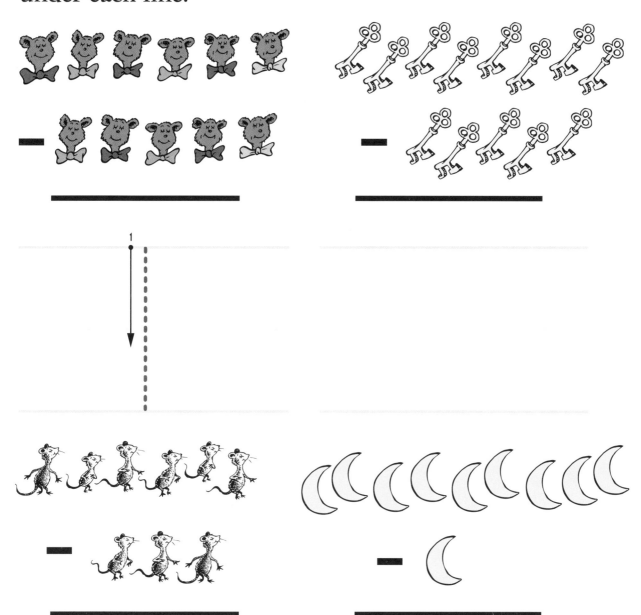

Write the Difference

Subtract the given numbers. Then color the picture using the colors that are assigned to each answer.

$$10 - 9 = \underline{\hphantom{0000}}$$
orange

$$9 - 7 = \underline{\hphantom{0000}}$$
red

$$7 - 4 = \underline{\hphantom{0000}}$$
yellow

$$5 - 1 = \underline{\hphantom{0000}}$$
green

$$8 - 3 = \underline{\hphantom{0000}}$$
blue

Subtraction

Hair We Go!

All kinds of hair, and all colors, too. Count and sort them.

_____ have blue hair.　　_____ have green hair.

_____ have pink hair.　　_____ have red hair.

How is your hair the same as people you know? How is it different? Draw a picture of all kinds of hair.

Skip Counting

There are other ways to count. Let's see how **5**s and **10**s make skip counting easy!

Count by **5**s. Color each fifth number blue.

1   2   3   4   5   6

7   8   9   10   11   12

13   14   15   16   17   18

Count by 10s. Color each tenth number red.

1   2   3   4   5   6

7   8   9   10   11   12

13   14   15   16   17   18

19   20   21   22   23   24

25   26   27   28   29   30

Counting by Fives

Counting by **5s**, fill in the missing numbers.

5   10   ___   20   ___

30   ___

50

___   ___

55   60   ___

70   ___   ___   85

___   95   100

Connect the dots, counting by 5s.
What do you see?

Counting by Tens

Counting by 10s, fill in the missing numbers.

10	20	30	___
___	60	___	80
90		___	110
	___	130	140
150	160	170	

Connect the dots, counting by 10s.
What do you see?

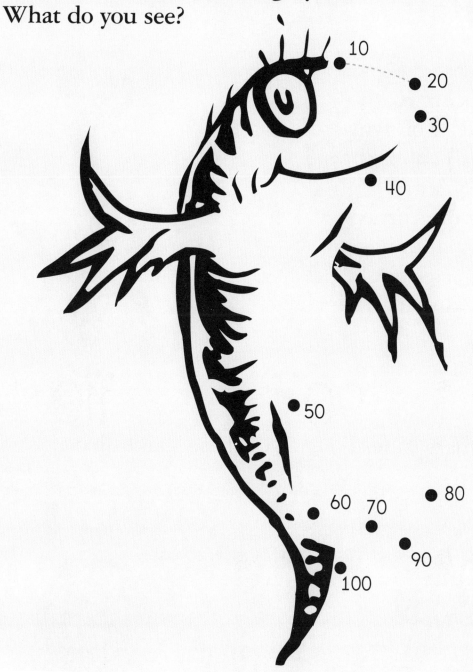

10
20
30
40
50
60 70 80
90
100

THING 1
THING 2

Skip Counting

YOU DID IT!

Shapes

Shapes are math—
we'll tell you why.
You can count the sides
if you just try.
Count the corners;
some shapes have many—
unless it's a circle,
which doesn't have any!

How many sides do each of these shapes have?

  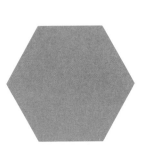

_____   _____   _____

Find four shapes hidden in the picture and color them.

Count the number of sides and corners for each shape you find.

Circles, Squares, Rectangles, and Triangles

This is a triangle. Trace it with your finger.
How many sides does it have? How many corners?

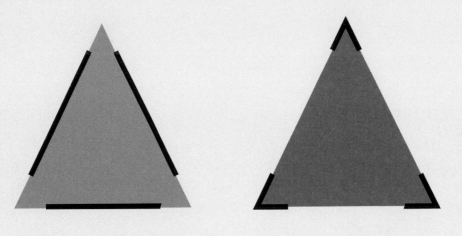

This is a square. Trace it with your finger.
How many sides does it have? How many corners?

This is a rectangle. Trace it with your finger.
How many sides does it have? How many corners?

This is a circle. Trace it with
your finger. It has no sides.
It has no corners.

Count all the shapes you see.

Rectangles: _____

Triangles: _____

Squares: _____

Circles: _____

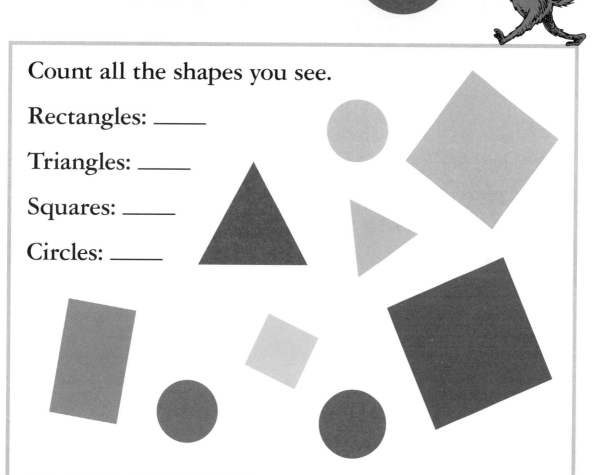

Pentagons, Hexagons, and Octagons

This is a pentagon. Trace it with your finger.
How many sides does it have? How many corners?

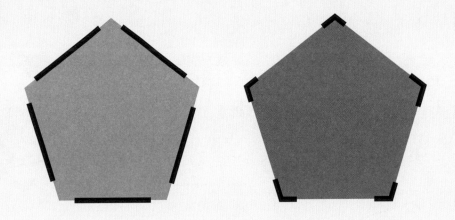

This is a hexagon. Trace it with your finger.
How many sides does it have? How many corners?

This is an octagon. Trace it with your finger.
How many sides does it have? How many corners?

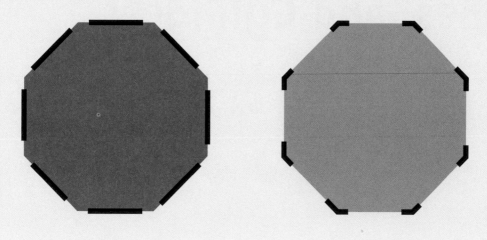

Color the pentagons red. Color the hexagons blue.
Color the octagons green.

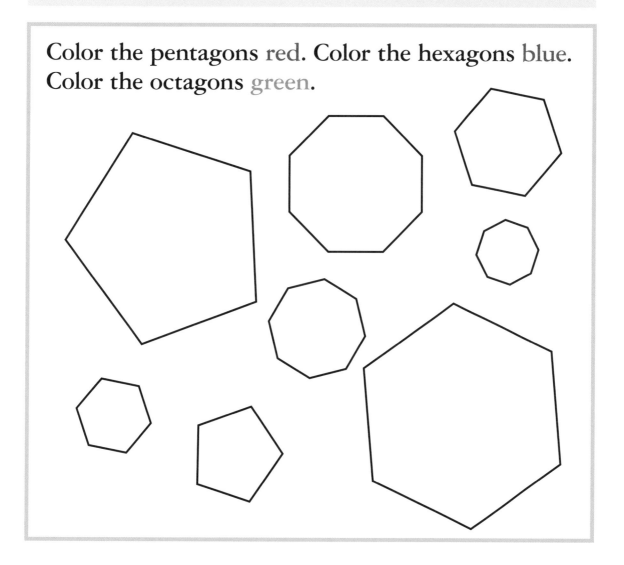

Cubes, Spheres, Cones, and Cylinders

Circles, triangles, and squares are flat. Since they have only two dimensions—length and width—they are called two-dimensional shapes.

Three-dimensional shapes have three dimensions—length, width, and depth.

A cube is shaped like a box.

A cylinder is shaped like a can.

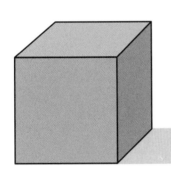

A sphere is shaped like a ball.

A cone is shaped like an ice cream cone!

Draw a line between the shapes that match.

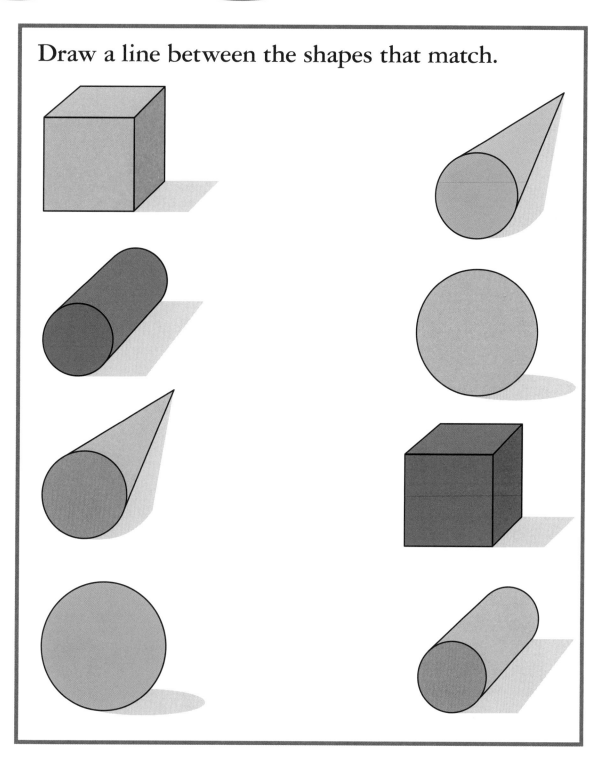

Shapes

YOU DID IT!

Sleepy Time

Everyone is yawning because they all need to sleep. Circle the biggest yawner. Draw a square around the littlest yawner.

Now keep track of YOUR sleep.
I went to bed at _____.
I woke up at _____.
I slept _____ hours.

Keep track a day later. If you slept differently, did you feel better or worse?

184

Certificate of Achievement

★ ★

is presented to

_____
NAME

for becoming a

Math Magician!

★ ★

Today you are YOU, that is TRUER than true. There is NO ONE alive who is YOU-ER than YOU.

Emotions

Sometimes you feel cheerful.
Sometimes you feel mad.
Our moods keep on changing,
from happy to sad.

Draw a picture of how you feel right now.

Write a word to describe each face's emotion.
Use the words in the word box to help you.

angry	happy	sad
proud	excited	scared

_____

_____

_____

_____

_____

Sad, Angry, Disappointed

How do you look when
you're sad? Draw it.

How do you look
when you're angry?
Draw it.

How do you look when
you're disappointed?
Draw it.

Draw a picture or write about something that made you feel angry.

Scared, Frustrated, Confused

How do you look when
you're scared? Draw it.

How do you
look when you're
frustrated? Draw it.

How do you look when
you're confused? Draw it.

Circle the word that matches each picture.

Scared

Frustrated

Confused

Scared

Frustrated

Confused

Scared

Frustrated

Confused

Proud, Excited, Happy

How do you look when
you're proud? Draw it.

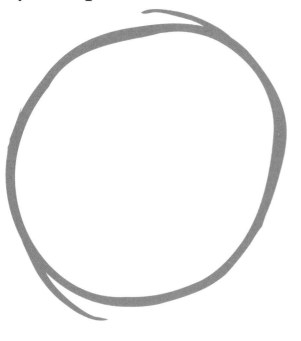

How do you look
when you're excited?
Draw it.

How do you look when
you're happy? Draw it.

Write the word that describes the feeling in each picture.

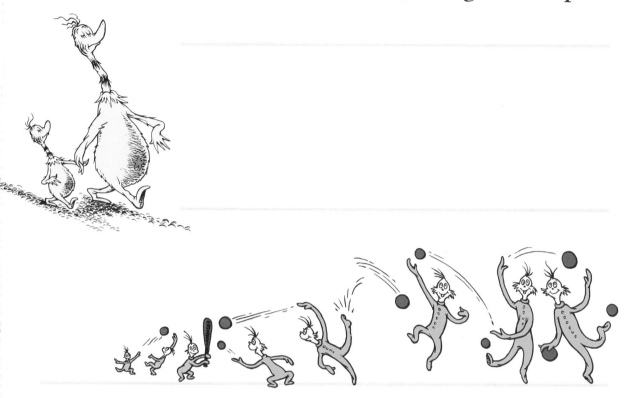

Expressing Feelings

Everyone expresses feelings in different ways.

When some people get angry, they yell—
but yelling can make other people feel sad.

There are things you can do when you're
angry that don't make someone else feel bad.

You can squeeze a pillow or
do jumping jacks instead.

It is good to talk
about how you feel.

How do you look when
you're surprised? Draw it.

How do you look when
you're tired? Draw it.

Draw something you can do when you're angry that wouldn't make someone else feel bad.

Identifying How Others Feel

How can you tell how
other people feel?
You can look at
their faces.
You can listen
to what they say.
You can watch
what they do.

If my friend was mad, I would _____

_____

_____

Draw a picture of what you could do if you saw that a friend was sad.

Emotions

YOU DID IT!

Getting Along!

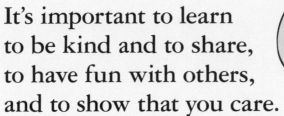

It's important to learn
to be kind and to share,
to have fun with others,
and to show that you care.

Circle the groups that are happily getting along.

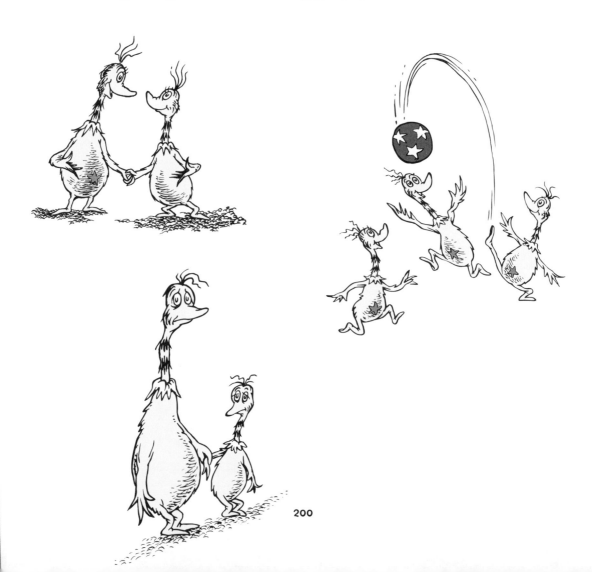

Put an X on the groups that
are not getting along.

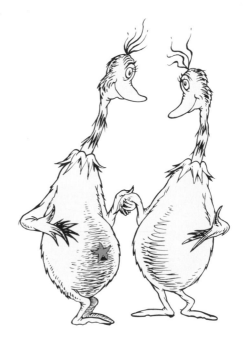

201

Sharing

It's nice to share your things with others. You don't have to share everything, though.

Draw or write about a time when you shared.

Draw one thing that you don't want to share.

Taking Turns

It's my turn. Now it's your turn. See?
Taking turns is easy to do. Circle 🖐 on the
picture that shows taking turns. Circle 🖐
on the picture that shows not taking turns.

Draw or write about a time when you took turns doing something.

Following the Rules

When you're inside, you use a quiet voice. When you're crossing a street, you look both ways first. There are different rules for different places.

Draw or write about one rule you have at home.

Draw or write about one rule you have at school.

Helping Out

When there's work to do, the job is easier if everyone pitches in.

Draw more birds to help carry the little one.

Draw a picture to show how you help out at home, then write about it below.

_____

_____

_____

_____

 **Getting Along!**

Sing a Song All Day Long

Letters tell us the sounds in words.
Notes  tell us the sounds in music.
Circle the music notes in the picture.

Make up a funny song to sing, then
teach it to a friend.

We Have So Much in Common

Is your hair straight or curly?
Are your eyes brown or blue?
There is no one around
who's exactly like you.
We are all very different,
but, also, it's true:
We have so much in common,
me, he, she, and you!

Circle all the things these two have in common.

Draw or write about the ways in which you are the same as each person pictured below.

The Things We All Need

We all need food.

We all need rest.

Draw another thing we all need.

Circle the things that everyone needs, then write a few more things that you need.

I need _____

_____

_____

Our Families!

Some families are big.

Some families are small.

How many people are in your family? _____

Draw a picture of your family.

I Like Being Different

Circle the one that is different from the rest.
What makes it different?

What is something special that makes you different from the people you know? Draw or write about it.

We Have So Much in Common

YOU DID IT!

Solving Problems

If you're faced with a problem
that you don't understand,
you better start thinking
before it gets out of hand.
Think of what would be better,
think of what would be best,
then dream up a plan
and follow the steps.
And if you can't solve
the problem all on your own,
find someone to help you—
you're never alone!

Write about a problem you had and how you solved it.

_____

_____

_____

_____

_____

Draw a line to match each problem with a solution.

Identifying the Problem

What problem does the person in the picture have?

_____

_____

_____

Draw a picture that shows a good way
to solve this problem.

Looking for Lots of Solutions

Some problems are easy to solve.

Some problems are not easy to solve. Then you have to use your noodle to think of ways to solve it.

You can ask other people for help—two noodles are better than one!

Write the names of three people you might ask to help you if you needed to solve a problem.

_____

_____

_____

Draw or write about how you could work together to find a solution to a problem.

Finding Solutions That Work for Everyone

There are some ways to solve a problem that make one person happy but another person sad, angry, or disappointed.

That's not a good solution.

A good solution works for everyone.

There are four friends and only two pieces of pizza left. Two people could eat a slice, and two people could have none. Is that a good solution?

How would you solve the problem?

Draw your solution, then complete the sentence.

A good solution would be to _____

_____

_____

_____

Solving Problems

YOU DID IT!

I Like Me!

I like myself.
Of course I do.
If you knew me well,
you'd like me, too.

Write a word that describes one thing Horton could be proud of.

Draw a picture of yourself doing something you are good at.

All About Me

Write about something everyone knows about you.

Everyone knows that I _____

_____

_____

_____

_____

Write about something that only a few people
know about you.

Only a few people know that I _____

_____

_____

_____

_____

Things That Make Me Special

How many ways are you special? There are too many to count!

Circle the creature who looks proud.

Draw a picture of some things that make you special.

I Like Me!

YOU DID IT!

Build Your Skills

What are these birds building?
Draw their creation in the empty space.

Now design and build something yourself.

Draw a picture. Then gather strings,
sticks, and blocks…and make it!

Likes and Needs

I like eating ice cream.
I like it a lot.
But do I need ice cream?
No, I do not.
I need air to breathe
and water to drink,
a warm place to sleep
and a place that's quiet
to sit and think.

Write a sentence about something you need.

I need _____

_____

_____

Draw a picture of something you like.

Likes and Dislikes

It's okay to like things that other people dislike. It's also okay to dislike things that other people like.

Put an X on at least one thing that you dislike.

Circle at least one thing that you like.

Needs and Wants

Food is something you need. Dessert is something you want. Can you tell the difference?

Draw a picture of something you need.

Using the word box, write each thing in the correct column.

| water | air | candy | toys | a home |
| vacation | rest | food | television | clothes |

needs

_____

_____

_____

_____

_____

_____

wants

_____

_____

_____

_____

_____

_____

Having Patience

Sometimes you want something that you can't have right away.

That's when you need to have patience.

Having patience isn't easy, but there are ways to make waiting lots of fun.

Circle the things you think would be fun to do while you wait.

Thumb wrestle

Make up a silly song

Look for everything that is purple

Play a guessing game with a friend

Draw or write some more fun things you can do while you wait.

Likes and Needs

YOU DID IT!

Certificate of Achievement

is presented to

NAME

for becoming a

Fantastic Friend!

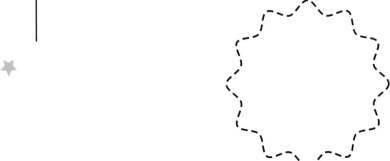

SCIENCE

Think and
WONDER. Wonder
and THINK.
How much WATER
can fifty-five
elephants
DRINK?

Earth and Space

The planet Earth goes around in space.

It really is a perfect place.

Trace the first letter of each planet.

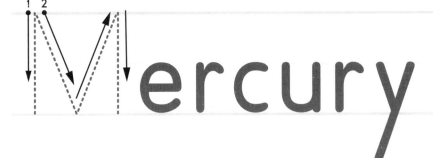

 Mercury

 Venus

 Earth

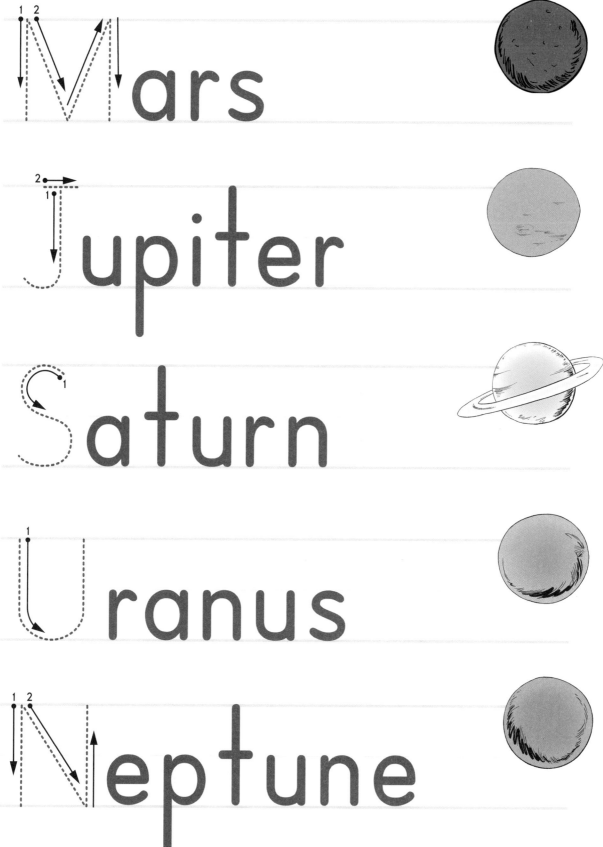

Mars

Jupiter

Saturn

Uranus

Neptune

Can you say them all in one breath?

The Planets

Color Earth blue and green.

Color the other planets.

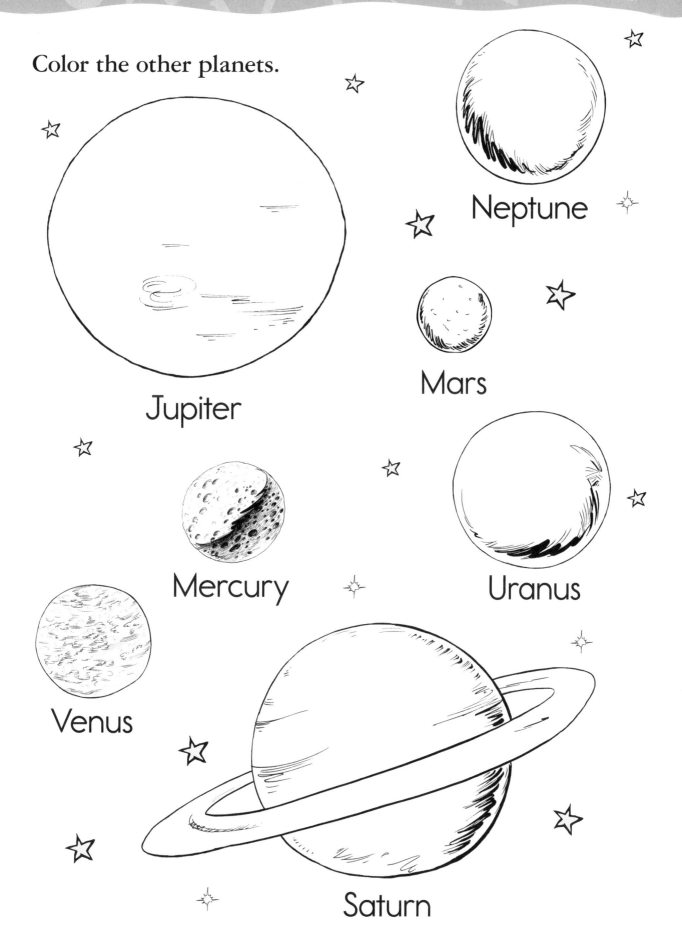

Jupiter

Neptune

Mars

Mercury

Uranus

Venus

Saturn

Day and Night

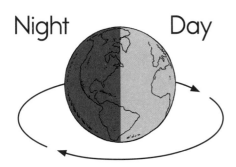

Night   Day

Circle all the things that can spin like the Earth.

Draw someone who runs and plays when the sun is out during the day.

Draw someone who comes out when the moon is up at night.

Landforms

Draw some very tall mountains.

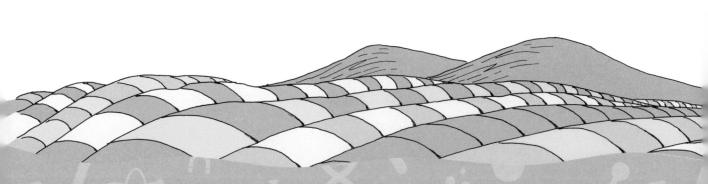

Draw a path to the island.

Weather

Trace, then write each weather word.

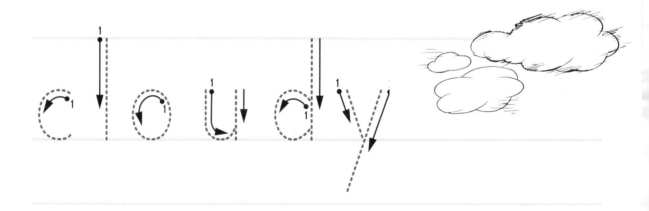

rainy

snowy

windy

Climate

Climate is what the weather is like in an area over a long period of time.

Some places, like the desert, have a hot, dry climate. Circle the things that belong in a desert.

Others, like the rain forest, have a hot, wet climate. Circle the things that belong in a rain forest.

What is the climate like where you live?
Draw and write about it.

_____

_____

_____

_____

Earth and Space

Push Me, Pull You

What are they using to push the elephant onto the scale? Draw something that can help them.

Look around you. Find two things that you must push to make it work.

Find one thing you must pull to make it work.

Life Science

I am alive—and so are you.

We eat, we breathe,
we move around, too!

Circle those who are eating.
Circle those who are moving.

Draw a picture of a living thing.

Living and Nonliving

Circle all the living things.

Put an X on all the nonliving things.

Babies Grow

Living things grow and change.

Draw a path to help the puppy reach its parent.

Draw a line between each baby and its parent.

Living Things: What Plants Need to Grow

Plants are alive. They need water and sunlight to grow.

What kinds of plants would you like to grow? Draw them in this empty garden.

Circle the things that plants need to grow.

Living Things: What Animals Need to Grow

Animals, including people, are living things.

Draw paths to what the bear needs to survive.

Here are some things that you need to survive.

Draw one more.

Habitats

The place where a living thing lives
is called its habitat.

Draw something that might live in this habitat.

Draw a line between the living thing and its habitat.

Life Science

Health

Your health is important,
and healthy food is the best,
not to mention exercise
and getting plenty of rest.

Draw paths to the foods that can keep you healthy.

Draw a picture of a way you stay healthy,
then write about it.

Your Body

Trace, then write each word.

leg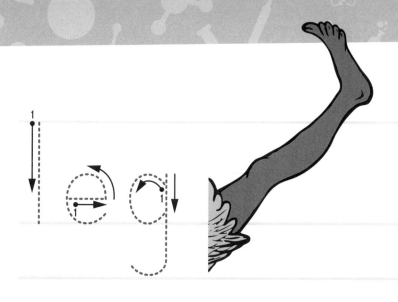

hair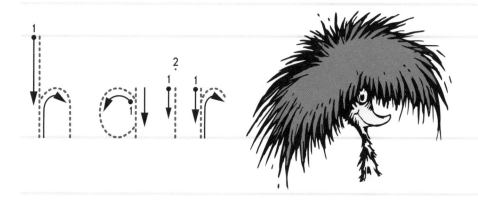

hand

Healthy Foods

Healthy food helps your body work better.
Draw some healthy, tasty food on this plate.

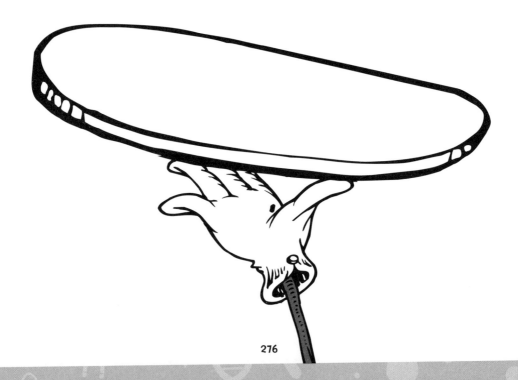

Circle the healthy foods you can eat.

Exercise

Exercise helps your body work better, too.

Circle everyone who is exercising.

Draw a picture that shows something you can do to exercise, then get up and do it!

Staying Safe

Circle the things that would protect this skater.

Circle the things that keep you safe.

Wash! Wash! Wash!

Wash, wash, wash your hands—gently, with some soap! Color two bubbles pink. Color three bubbles green.

Wash your hands and sing a splish-splash song while you do it! You can use the tune of "Row, Row, Row Your Boat" or you can make up your own tune. Make sure your song is at least 30 seconds long.

Physical Science

A rock, a brick, a house, a bike.
Here are some ways they're all alike:
They do not eat. They do not grow.
They're not alive, that's why it's so.

Put an X on everything that moves.

Circle the word that matches each thing.

living   nonliving

living   nonliving

living   nonliving

living   nonliving

living   nonliving

living   nonliving

Pushes and Pulls

Nonliving things can't move on their own. You have to use energy to move them.

Circle the things you can push. Put an X on the things you can pull.

Where could you get the energy to push or pull something? Draw it here.

Magnets

Magnets are special things that can push
or pull some kinds of metal.

Circle all the things that are magnetic.

Draw something that's made of metal that this magnet is lifting.

Solids and Liquids

A solid keeps its shape.
For example, an ice cube is a solid.

A liquid takes the shape of its container.
For example, water is a liquid.

A gas fills a container.
For example, steam from a teapot is a gas.

Circle the word that is a gas.

land   air   sea

Draw a picture of something that is liquid.

Color all the things that are solid.

Sink and Float

Flowers and other light things float on water.

Rocks and other heavy things sink in water.

Circle the things that would float in water.

Put an X on the things that would sink in water.

Physical Science

Taking Care of Our World

From a little black ant
to a huge polar bear,
this planet is one
that all living things share.

We all have to care for it—
you can pitch in.
And if you haven't yet started,
it's time to begin!

Draw a path to someone who is working
to take care of the planet.

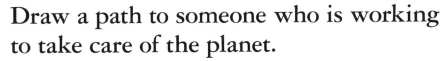

Draw something you can do to take care of the Earth, then write about it below.

_____

_____

_____

_____

All the Green Things

Our planet needs plants, shrubs, and trees.

They give animals food and homes.
They help keep our air clean.

Finish the city by filling it with trees and other plants.

Circle all the plants.

Taking Out the Trash

Trash isn't good for our planet.

That's why it's important to recycle things like glass bottles, plastic containers, tin cans, cardboard boxes, and paper.

Draw a path to properly take out the recycling.

Can you reuse these pieces of junk? Draw new, useful objects using these old, discarded pieces.

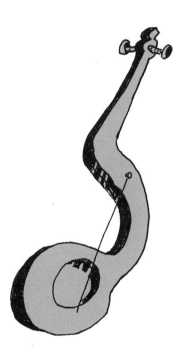

Energy Savers

We use energy to turn on a light or talk on the phone. We use Earth's resources to make energy. Some of them can't be replaced.

Circle everything in this picture that uses energy.

Draw a picture of a way that you can save energy.

Taking Care of Our World

YOU DID IT!

Tweetle Beetles in a Bottle

It's a tweetle beetle bottle puddle paddle battle muddle! How many tweetle beetles are in the bottle?

Now go outside and look for living things that are even smaller than a tweetle beetle.

Where do they live? What are they doing?

Draw a picture of one, and write a sentence about what it is doing.

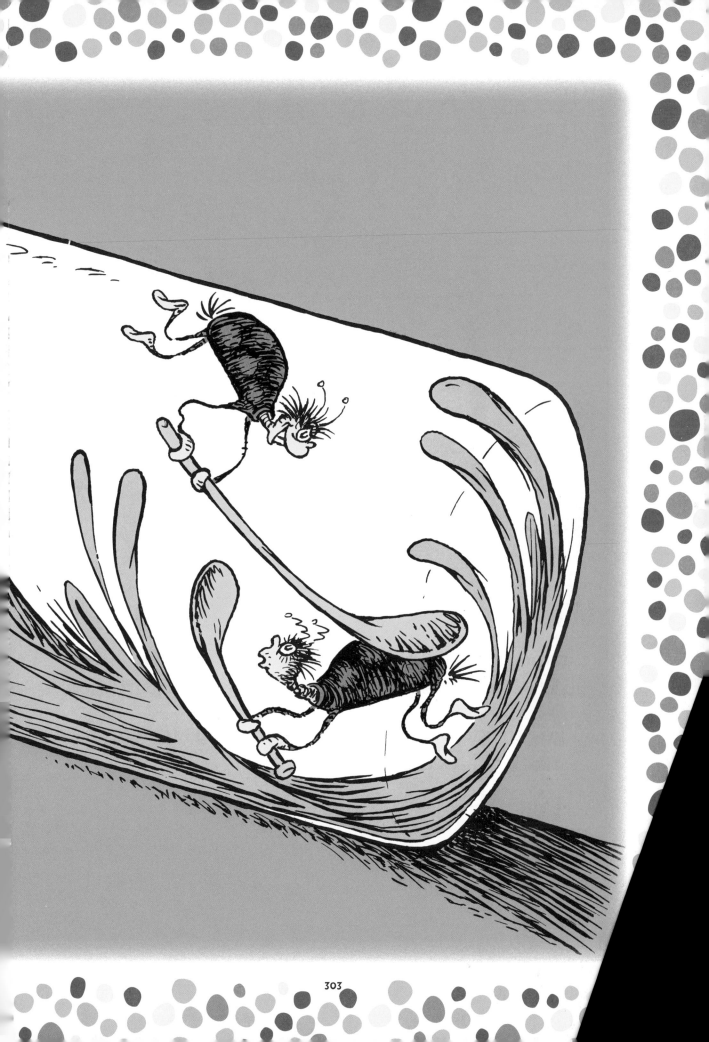

Certificate of Achievement ★ ★

is presented to

_____

NAME

for becoming a

Science Superstar!